EMMA CUT
RUBY KAN

BLAZED WAX

Creating sculptural
candles for any space

Hardie Grant

BOOKS

A candle transforms any space. It delights the senses by the
way it looks and smells. It can wake you up, help you to
relax, set the mood or get you in the mood. Candles bring
to life a dinner table, a picnic or a special event. They evoke
stories and memories among friends and family. They can
create excitement, such as blowing out a candle on top of a
cake. Candles signify celebrations, delicious food, religious
ceremonies, gatherings of friends, remembering ones lost.
There's something innately magical about the way a candle
burns and brings us together.

Candle-making for us is not only our job but a fun and therapeutic pastime. We find such great enjoyment from experimenting, mixing colours and discovering what we have created in the end. Making candles is a great way to explore your creativity in a sculptural but also functional way. We still love to buy beautiful candles created by other makers, but it is fun and satisfying to be able to DIY them too, especially when you burn through them as fast as we do!

As candle appreciators and makers, we've loved discovering great tips in candle books from the '90s that we've found hidden in the back of second-hand shops, covered in cobwebs. But we soon realised there are few candle-making resources on interesting, contemporary and sculptural candles. We want to show you how to create candles that you will truly love (not like the angel-shaped ones you get given for your work Secret Santa). So if you love to burn beautiful candles as much as we do, this is the book you have been waiting for!

Don't panic, making candles is not as hard as you may think. We promise we are great teachers. In fact, Emma *is* a teacher, and Ruby may as well be because she teaches Emma

so much! This book is a step-by-step guide, with easy-to-understand instructions and gorgeous pictures to aid and inspire your candle journey. You will be amazed at the many shapes you can mould and colours you can create.

The key to sculptural candle-making is experimentation. The activities in this book are merely a guide; you can modify any of them as you wish. One of the reasons we absolutely love wax as a medium is because if you make a mistake or something goes wrong, you can just melt it down and start again. Not only does that mean candle-making is a cost-effective craft, it's also super sustainable as there is not a lot of waste.

Learning the ancient art of candle-making – but with a modern twist – will bring a new love and appreciation to your candle obsession. You will feel a special connection and pride when giving these candles to your loved ones or placing them around your home. And however your candles turn out – wonky, straight or otherwise – it's about the journey. If you had fun trying something new with an activity in this book, then our job is done. We can't wait for you to get started!

SPARKS FLY

— RUBY AND EMMA

We have been friends for more than ten years – some might call us twin flames. We met at a music festival, having a boogie in a field under the Milky Way. A big part of our friendship is our love for all things creative. Emma studied fashion and runs her own clothing label; Ruby studied fine art and runs her own jewellery label.

We share a studio space and also a home – a big, old Californian bungalow in Melbourne, where we live with our matching poodles, Bilbo and Beanie. We love styling our home with candles made by us and by others – we find an eclectic mix is what makes a wonderful space. We have a large collection of candles lugged home from trips to Mexico, India, Italy, Greece and the United States, which takes pride of place on our shelves. Our house is also filled with beautiful candelabras and candlestick holders, most of which we have found at local second-hand and vintage shops.

We follow creative pursuits together, including still-life painting, mosaics and ceramics (Emma is great on the wheel and Ruby paints the fired product). During the COVID-19 lockdowns of 2020, one of the many activities we immersed ourselves in was candle-making, and we fell in love with it straight away. We loved it so much that we wanted to start sharing it with others. Emma brought her styling and business skills, Ruby brought her artistic and sculptural background, we experimented and researched, and our first co-venture, Blazed Wax, was born.

Our love for candles goes beyond styling. We are both from European families, and a huge part of our cultures is sitting together over food and being proud of our table presentation. We both grew up in small rural towns, where the power would frequently go out, and there was nothing more exciting than sitting around by candlelight during a blackout, waiting for someone to turn the generator back on.

We especially love to cook and host dinners for friends, filling the table with an abundance of candles and flowers. It makes every meal special, elevated by flickering light. The ritual of dressing the table to share food with the ones we love has been the cornerstone of our friendship.

The most beautiful thing about making candles together is the merging of our ideas and talents: learning from and inspiring each other. This collaboration is the pillar (pun intended) of our venture together.

Know your candles

Sculptural (mould) candles

Dinner candles

Scented candles

Pillar candles

Birthday candles

Taper (hand-dipped) candles

PART ONE

GETTING STARTED

SAFETY FIRST

We know it seems obvious, but candle safety is a must, especially when crafting with hot wax ... very hot wax!

Ensure you have a safe working space, as you'll be using a source of heat. We have a portable butane gas burner, which you can get from the camping section of your local hardware store, or you can use your stovetop at home. Always make sure you have a fire blanket or extinguisher, a clear working area with an even surface, access to water, and proper ventilation.

Spend a few minutes setting up your workspace properly. Wax is messy and can go everywhere. We always lay down old cardboard boxes or newspaper on the surface and floor so we can keep refreshing our workspace when it gets too waxy. Candle-making requires patience (wax can take a few hours to dry), so don't rush any steps, including preperation.

Wear suitable clothing, such as an apron or art smock, and closed-toed shoes. Your clothes will most likely get wax on them, and it's a pain to get out. Boiling water is the best way to remove wax stains from your clothes or shoes, but always pour it outside. Soy wax is biodegradable, so it's not bad for the garden!

NEVER leave heating wax unattended, as it can ignite. If your wax starts to bubble or smoke, turn it off immediately and wait for it to cool. We always recommend the use of a digital thermometer when melting wax and making candles to avoid fire, burns and damage to your utensils and home. We once had an instance where the wax was way too hot and burnt a hole through a plastic jug when being poured from the pot. Luckily no one was hurt! Aside from potential injuries, if the temperature of the wax is too high, you get yucky bubbles in your candles. See pages 20–21 for more on wax safety.

Never tip wax down the sink! As soon as the wax gets cold it solidifies and can block your drain, so wait for it to set and put it in the bin instead.

LIT UP

Never leave a burning candle unattended! Always keep burning candles out of reach of kids and animals, away from anything flammable (such as curtains) and draughty areas (such as an open window or the pathway of a heater).

Never burn your candle for more than three hours at a time.

Always burn your candles on a heatproof surface – candles in jars can really heat up and wax can spill, causing damage to your furniture.

Always keep your wick trimmed to approximately 7 mm (⅓ in) for a safe flame.

MATERIAL WORLD

In this section you will find all the things you'll need to start
making candles. Candle-making can be a sustainable and
inexpensive hobby if done correctly. Everything we do
in life should respect our planet, and making candles is
no different. We know hobbies can come and go (not to
mention, the cost of buying lots of new things can add up
fast), so there's no need to go out and buy fancy-schmancy
tools and equipment when most can be thrifted or found
around the home.

For those items you can't thrift, such as wax and wicks, there
are lots of great candle-making supply stores. We buy a
lot of our materials online, but sometimes it helps to go
into a store to see, feel and smell the supplies and get the
professional opinion of the staff.

TAKEAWAY TREASURE

You know when you look into that cupboard filled with millions of old takeaway containers and jars you've collected over the years and wonder why you've kept them? This is why! Hurrah! We use old takeaway containers and jars for projects, and to store all of our hard dyes, wax, wicks and tools. If you can't find what you need from around the house, then look in thrift stores and second-hand shops.

Wax

Wax is the most important component of your candle. We don't often specify wax quantities in the book as they depend on the size of your mould or vessel, or how tall or wide you might want to make your hand-dipped candles. A good rule of thumb to measure for a mould or vessel is to fill it twice with wax chips, which should give you roughly the right amount to melt. It doesn't matter too much if you melt more than you need because you can always just allow it to set and then save it for next time to remelt.

There are various waxes available and each creates a completely different finished product. There are hundreds of brands of wax, made with different ingredients and compounds, so we recommend always doing some research into the particular brand of wax you will be using. But we can help with the basics.

SOY WAX is our favourite wax to work with. It's biodegradable and non-toxic. As long as you're certain your soy wax is 100 per cent natural, without the addition of any other toxic types of wax like paraffin, it's completely compostable. Plus it sets with a solid milky colour, meaning it is great for dyeing different colours. Soy wax is designed to sit in a candle jar where it stays in liquid form and burns for longer. It's not really designed for making pillar candles; it has a low melt temperature and doesn't evaporate, so it will be drippy and continue to change form in a range of shapes. You will also have to make sure you burn your free-standing soy wax candle on a surface that won't be ruined by melted wax, but if you're a thrifty sort, you can melt the excess wax down and reuse it. Keep in mind any charcoal bits may be visible in your new candle, so try to use only clean old wax.

If you are making a mould candle, we recommend using a pillar soy wax that is designed to contract and be pulled from a mould, as opposed to a container soy wax that will be too soft. Look for something that sets harder, most likely a blended product (see below). Please check with your supply store for more information.

SOY BLEND WAX is usually made of soy wax and paraffin wax, as well as other additives to make your wax act a certain way. Soy wax can also be blended with palm wax, coconut wax or beeswax. If you are working with a soy blend, your wax may not be compostable or biodegradable, so keep this in mind when disposing of old candles. You may want to look into using a soy blend when making candles from a silicone mould, as soy wax will need an additive to ensure it keeps its shape.

STORING WAX

Storing your waxes in a cool, dark place will preserve their quality of your waxes and keep them from being damaged. Always store them out of direct sunlight and under 27 °C (80 °F). Remember to keep your waxes tightly sealed – if you get dust in your wax, you will get dust in your candles. Devote certain containers to holding similar coloured waxes, so you don't get any surprise bits of unwanted colour in your finished candle.

THE THING ABOUT PALM WAX

Palm wax has a high melting point and is
a cost-effective choice, but it has led to
deforestation in Indonesia and Malaysia, so
it's damaging to the environment. We don't
use palm wax for this reason, and we don't
recommend you use it either.

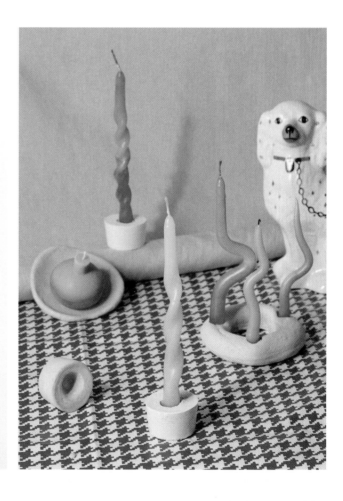

PARAFFIN WAX is ideal for holding the shape of pillar candles or moulds; however, it is made from petroleum and releases toxic chemicals when burnt. Paraffin isn't compostable and what remains after a candle is burnt will have to be thrown in the bin. As the majority of your candle will evaporate into the air, this isn't a huge problem for landfill, but the toxins may be inhaled by you and your family, so keep this in mind. When paraffin wax sets it becomes slightly translucent, which is a lovely effect and looks quite different to soy.

BEESWAX is a natural wax produced by honeybees. It has a honey fragrance and colour, which emits a warm glow when burnt. Beeswax is very dense and has a higher melting point than other waxes, meaning it burns slower and drips less. Beeswax is a great base for a scented candle – you can add natural oils to it or leave it as is for a beautiful alternative to artificially scented candles. The best thing about beeswax is that it acts as an air purifier! Burning beeswax releases negative ions, which then attach themselves to positive ions in the air (such as dust, mould, odour, toxins) and cancel them out, essentially cleaning the air around you. Cool, huh!?

COCONUT WAX is non-toxic, biodegradable and sustainable, as it is obtained via a completely natural process, has a high crop renewal and is high yield per acre. Candles made from coconut wax are clear-burning and have a lovely scent. Coconut wax is one of the slowest burning waxes, which gives your candle a much longer burn time than others. It works well when mixed with oils and burns best in a jar.

COLOURED WAX SHEETS are flat pieces of wax, similar to a sheet of paper, used for modelling, shaping and decorating your candles. These wax sheets come in paraffin wax and beeswax.

Digital thermometer

Don't risk a burn: make sure a digital thermometer is one of the first items you add to your cart when you're purchasing candle-making supplies. Digital thermometers are also handy in the kitchen, so they're a worthy purchase.

Believe it or not, the pouring temperature can make or break your stunning new candle creation. Trust us, we know! Trying to rush to the finish line will leave you further behind than the tortoise. Taking time to test the temperature of your wax will save your candle's life in the long run.

If the wax is too hot, aside from the dangers (you could be splattered with boiling wax or the wax might melt through the plastic of your pouring jug), bubbles will form in your candle that can then appear on its surface. If your wax isn't hot enough, you will get textured lines through it.

Remember, never leave hot wax unattended, and ALWAYS check the temperature of your wax is within the recommended temperatures (see opposite) before pouring it into a jug or container.

POURING TEMPERATURES

Soy wax: 70–75 ºC (160–165 ºF)

Paraffin wax: 65 ºC (150 ºF)

Soy blend wax: 50–55 ºC (120–130 ºF)

Beeswax: 70 ºC (160 ºF)

Wicks

Selecting the correct wick for your candle can be tricky. As a general rule, smaller candles need thinner wicks and bigger candles need thicker wicks. If the wick is too big, it will burn too fast for the candle, and you will be left with a puddle of wax before your very eyes. If the wick is too small, the wax will pool and put out your flame. You need a flame that is going to sustain the melting of the wax, but not go too hard. We suggest you try out different wick sizes depending on your candle, especially when experimenting with sculptural shapes.

Some wicks are pre-coated in a layer of wax, which is extremely helpful when using moulds as it's easier to thread your wick through your wick hole. Pre-coated wicks come in set lengths – when choosing the correct wick length, you generally want to allow an additional 5 cm (2 in) over your mould, vessel or desired hand-dipped candle height. Then you can trim the wick to approximately 7 mm (⅓ in) before you burn the candle.

Uncoated cotton wicks don't come in pre-cut lengths and are also more flexible, so they will give you more freedom to experiment with funky shapes and sizes. Most good candle-making supply stores will guide you through the best wicks for your chosen wax and candle shape. You can also pre-wax a wick yourself by fully submerging it in wax once, then allowing it to set while laid flat and straight.

THINK STRAIGHT

Keeping your wick straight is the most important part of getting your candle to burn evenly. Hot glue or wick tabs can be used attached to the bottom of a jar or container to stop the bottom of your wick from moving (some pre-coated wicks will have wick tabs already attached). You can also purchase metal wick straighteners to sit at the top of the jar or mould to keep the top of the wick in place. However, humble clothes pegs and popsicle sticks can be used just as easily for this (our preferred method). After making candles for a little while you will determine what tools work best for you.

Moulds

Mould-making can be messy, complicated and time-consuming, but it is also a lot of fun and means that your candle will be entirely unique. The best thing about learning how to make your own candle moulds is that you can use just about anything in the house. Love the shape of your soy sauce bottle? Make a candle out of it! It's also fun to go thrifting and buy little trinkets that would otherwise sit there for years collecting dust, and turn them into an amazing candle.

To create our moulds, we use two-part silicone. We'll walk through the process of creating and pouring a mould candle in the first projects, on pages 32–45.

Certain shapes are more complicated to mould than others, so to start with choose something that is symmetrical and either a consistent width or tapered on the ends. Don't choose anything that is too wonky or oddly shaped (we can get to that later). The texture of the object you want immortalised in silicone will be replicated exactly in your mould, so keep that in mind.

If you don't want to make your own mould, there is a vast range available for purchase online. Most of the projects in this book can be made with pre-bought moulds – you can still put your own personal stamp on them.

REUSE, REMOULD

Silicone moulds only have a short life; they can be used about 10 times before they lose their lustre and start to grip on to the wax when pulling candles, often breaking the candle in the process. Silicone is expensive and not great for the environment, as it's essentially plastic. Luckily, you can reuse your old moulds or make new moulds, because old silicone bonds with new silicone. Cut your old moulds into tiny pieces and use them to fill the new mould, adding some new silicone to bond it all together.

COLOUR CHART

Red + blue = **deep purple**

Pink + blue = **lilac**

Green + yellow = **lime**

Green + blue = **teal**

Red + yellow = **orange**

Yellow + pink = **peach**

Brown + orange = **tan**

**BURNING THE CANDLE
AT BOTH ENDS**

Sometimes candles can crack when you're
pulling them, or funny marks appear on
them from a previous coloured wax that has
remained on the inside of your mould. Never
fear! Just melt them down and start again.

Dyes

Colours are our favourite part of making a
candle! To build your candle dye collection,
we suggest starting with primary colours. We
have provided some basic colour formulas
opposite, but experiment with the brand of
dye you buy and the ratios of each colour to
get varying shades. We always test coloured
wax in a white paper cup, and allow it to
harden before we pour our candle, so we
don't get any surprises later! The wax can
look really different when heated compared
to when it's cooled and set.

We use a combination of both liquid and
solid dyes to get a wide range of colours.

SOLID DYES can be easily and safely
stored in plastic containers, but you have to
melt them over heat, so one pot of wax can
only make one colour.

LIQUID DYES are messy – if you have a
spill, you will be trying to clean it off things
for weeks. The best thing about liquid
dyes, though, is that you can melt a big
pot of uncoloured wax, divide the wax into
containers and then add the dyes, so you
can get lots of colours from one melted pot.
You also get more bang for your buck as
the pigments are higher, meaning you need
a lot less dye, and one drop will give you a
completely different colour to three drops.
For example, our favourite blue dye will give
you a lovely pale baby blue with a single drop,
compared to three or four drops, which will
give you a deep indigo.

Scents

Aside from creating a beautiful glow, ambience and mood lighting, candles can excite your sense of smell! Scent is the strongest tie to memory, and different smells can really set your mood. We all have particular fragrances that remind us of a happy memory or make us feel calm and nurtured.

The impact of burning a scented candle can change the feeling of your entire home. We are so quick to make our spaces visually appealing, but why don't we spend time working on the smells in our home? There's nothing better than when someone walks into your house and tells you how good it smells. It's about the feeling as well as the aesthetics.

You can purchase synthetic scents for your candles, but we always opt for essential oils, which are naturally extracted from plants. They also don't create a huge scent throw, which means they're not overpowering,

instead giving off a subtle, natural scent. Having essential oils burning around the home is not only pleasurable on the nose, it can also help you relax, aid you in sleep and calm your nerves and anxieties. Keep in mind some scents are bad for pets, so look into this before purchasing.

When using essential oils it's important to remember if you use too much, your candle won't set properly and may crack, but if you use too little, you won't smell it. Our general rule of thumb is 15–20 ml to every 500 g of wax (½–¾ fl oz to every 17 oz). You may want to use a little more or less depending on your desired strength of smell.

Only add essential oils once the melted wax has cooled slightly – if the wax is too hot, the oils will burn off.

SCENTS WE LOVE

Lavender is well known for its calming and stress-relieving properties. We love to burn a lavender mix at home when we are winding down. Lavender is said to help with sleep and rest, so consider having a lavender-scented candle burning next to your bath or in your bedroom.

Peppermint will give you a kick of energy. We love to have some peppermint burning when we are doing chores or cleaning the house for a fresh feeling.

Bergamot is a wonderful oil for stress relief. Burn a bergamot-scented candle while you are running yourself a bath after a long day.

Sandalwood may have anti-inflammatory benefits, as well as a calming smell that can help manage anxiety. It's perfect for a lazy morning or a Sunday afternoon.

Ylang ylang boosts your mood and alleviates anxiety and depression.

Rose geranium calms and relaxes you. It also has antibacterial properties.

Clary sage is known to help with menstrual cramps! It can also reduce anxiety and calm the mind.

Patchouli helps to aid relaxation and reduces feelings of anxiety.

OUR FAVOURITE COMBINATIONS

Bergamot + clary sage

Rose geranium + patchouli + lavender

Ylang ylang + rose geranium

Other essential tools

Stovetop and pot to melt wax

Plastic jug to pour wax

Spoon or chopsticks to stir wax and silicone

Jars and vessels to hold candles, make moulds and generally be useful

Cardboard to make moulds and protect your work surfaces

Hot glue gun and glue to keep objects in place when making moulds or to attach wicks to vessels for scented candles (you can also use wick tabs for this)

Scissors to cut cardboard, trim wicks and open packets

Measuring cups and digital scales to measure out wax or silicone

Skewers (or a drill and small drill bit) to make wick holes in moulds

Sticky tape for sealing up any holes when making a mould

Scalpel or box cutter to cut your mould to help pull your object or candle out

Clothes pegs and popsicle sticks (or a wick-straigthening tool) to straighten your wicks

Paper cups to test dyed wax colours in

Elastic bands to hold any cuts in a mould tightly closed when pouring a candle

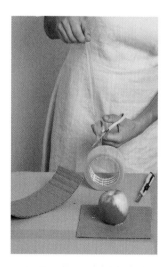

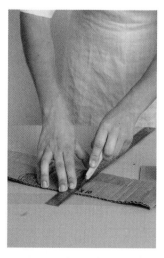

EXPRESS YOURSELF

There are so many places to find inspiration for your candle projects. Our biggest inspiration is travel. When we were travelling through Mexico together, we fell in love with the heavily stocked prayer shops next to all the Catholic churches. You could hardly move in these little stores – they were packed sky-high with candles of different sizes, colours and styles. They were reminiscent of the religious prayer candles Ruby grew up with, watching her Yiayia in Greek Orthodox churches (especially around Easter time), but in such bright beautiful colours. We brought home so many and had to carry them on the plane with us, so they didn't break in our check-in luggage.

Think about the style of your home. Do you want to match your candle to a piece of art? Do you want to add a pop of colour to your home with a bright and cheerful candle? Or do you want to add a sense of calm to your space?

Make a candle specifically with another person in mind. If you are gifting your candle, consider what the recipient likes. Ruby's mum loves rose geranium, so we always make sure we put a good splash of it in any candle being made for her, whereas Emma's mum loves lavender. We have other friends who are minimalists, so we may keep things monochrome for them.

PART ONE

PROJECTS

TUTTI FRUTTI

SIMPLE MOULD CANDLE

Let's start simple! An apple or citrus fruit is an excellent
  choice for moulding that you can probably find in your
  home. Fruit is cheap, it doesn't matter if it breaks, and it's
  small and symmetrical, which is ideal when you're first
  learning how to use silicone and pull a candle from a mould.
  We love the subtle texture you get with citrus fruit: every
  tiny bump comes up on the mould, and if you get the colour
  right when pouring it, your candle can look so similar to a
  real piece of fruit!
This project includes the basic 'recipe' for many of our
  candle-making projects. Once you have mastered this
  technique, you can go on to try other, more complex
  variations. And don't forget, always refer to our safety
  instructions on page 12 before making a candle!

Making the mould

YOU WILL NEED

~ An apple or other small piece of fruit

~ Two pieces of cardboard: a smaller piece to use as a base and a larger piece

~ Two-part silicone mix: approximately 300 ml (10 oz)

! The silicone we use is a 1:1 two-part mix; you will need to use about 150 ml (5 oz) of each part to make just over 1 cup of silicone. Use your discretion with this: if you have a giant apple you might need to make a little more, or vice versa.

1. Glue the apple to the centre of the smaller cardboard 'base' using a hot glue gun. Make sure it is properly stuck down; if not, it will rise once the silicone is poured and you will ruin your mould. You can also put some thumb tacks through the bottom of the cardboard to attach the apple (alternatively use a nail or screw).

2. To create the 'wall' of the mould, cut the larger piece of cardboard into a rectangle that measures a little longer than the circumference of your apple and at least 2 cm (1 in) taller than the height. Press some small folds into the cardboard, to help it bend easily, then use it to encircle the apple. Make sure there is about 1 cm (½ in) between the wall and the apple all the way around; if there is more space between them, it will make the candle harder to pull. Glue the bottom edge of the cardboard wall to the base, completely sealing the join.

3. Follow the packet instructions to mix the two-part silicone in a jug with a spoon. The silicone we use needs to be mixed for about a minute in a slow, steady motion. If you mix the silicone too fast you will get air bubbles, which will show up in your mould.

4. Once the parts are completely combined in the jug, slowly and steadily pour the silicone into the cardboard mould. Keep your hand steady in one spot and pour from up high to minimise air bubbles. Pour until there's at least 1 cm (½ in) of silicone above the height of the apple. Leave any excess silicone to dry in the jug – do NOT tip it down the sink! Tap the sides of your freshly poured mould gently for about a minute; this should dislodge any air bubbles in your wet silicone.

5. Leave the mould to dry for a minimum of four hours (or follow the packet instructions) – we recommend you let it set overnight for the strongest mould.

6. Once the mould has completely dried, remove the cardboard from the sides and base. You will notice there is a hole in one side of the mould where the bottom of the apple will be visible – this is the top of your mould and where you will pour wax into later. You want this hole to be neat and round; you may need to cut a little bit of silicone away using a box cutter or scalpel, but be careful to avoid splitting the mould as you do this.

7. Push your fingers inside the top of the mould and pull it back gently, using your thumbs to push the apple out of the hole (see photo overleaf). It's good to practise doing this carefully, as you will be using this technique to pop out your candles as well!

8. To finish you will need to make the wick hole. Locate the most central part of the bottom of the mould and prick a hole there with a wooden skewer, going back and forth a few times to ensure a wick can fit through there later. If you have a drill with a small bit handy, you can use this instead.

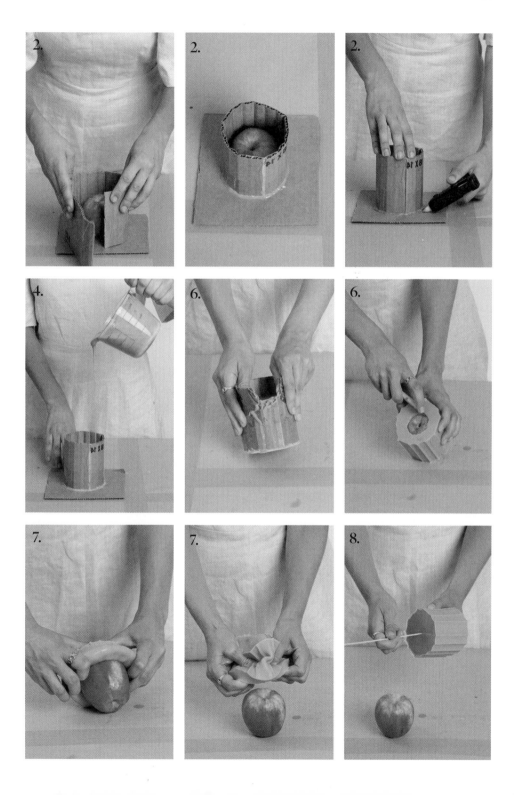

Making the candle

YOU WILL NEED

~ Coated wick (please refer to our wick guide on page 22)

~ Wax of your choice (we use a soy wax that is suitable for moulds; see page 16 for more information)

~ Your mould

~ Coloured dye of your choice (optional; otherwise keep your candle white or a natural honey colour if using beeswax)

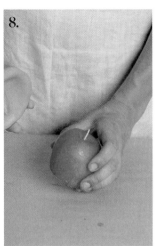
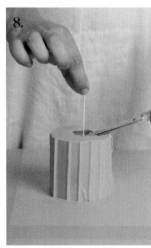

1. Take the wick and thread it into the wick hole of your mould. Set the mould aside on some newspaper or cardboard, in case you have any spills.

2. Place the wax chips into a pot and melt to the required temperature (see the ranges specified on page 21). Mix until the wax has all melted.

3. If using a dye, add it to the wax and mix well. If using dye chips, ensure the dye is dissolved completely.

4. Using a digital thermometer, check the temperature of the wax to ensure it won't burn through a plastic jug and you won't get air bubbles in your candles.

5. Transfer the melted wax into a plastic jug, then slowly pour the wax into your mould, until it reaches just under the lip of the top opening.

6. Ensure the wick is centred and peg it into place, letting the peg rest on the top of the mould. You can also use a wick-straightening tool.

7. Allow to set for around five hours, or until the candle is completely cool to touch. If you try to pull the candle too early it will break, so be patient.

8. Push your fingers inside the top of the mould and pull it back gently, using your thumbs to push the apple out of the hole. Finally, trim the wick.

! If you are having trouble pulling your candle from the mould, it might be because the silicone is too thick and not flexible enough. To solve this problem, take a scalpel or box cutter and carefully cut away any excess silicone in the areas that feel too thick. Go slow with this – if you pierce your mould, you will have to make another one.

SALT N' PEPPER

SCULPTURAL MOULD CANDLE

Now that you've mastered the apple or citrus candle, perhaps you want to try making a taller candle in a more complex shape. A pepper grinder or small vase have interesting shapes and can easily be found around the home or in a thrift shop. These objects can be difficult to remove from your mould, so we will show you how to cut the mould to enable you to safely remove the object and candle without breaking them.

Making *the* mould

YOU WILL NEED

~ A vase or pepper grinder (or other interesting vessel)

~ Two pieces of cardboard: a smaller piece to use as a base and a larger piece

~ Two-part silicone mix (amount will depend on the size of the vessel)

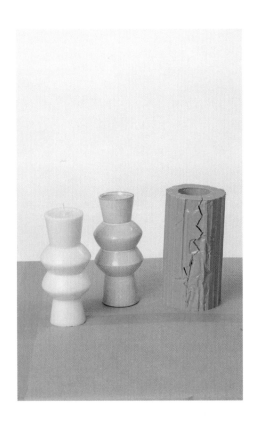

1. If your vase/grinder has a hole in the top, you will need to seal this using sticky tape. If you are having trouble making the tape grip, use hot glue to stick the tape down. Keep in mind any bumps will come up in your mould, so use a scalpel or box cutter to trim down any bits of glue to make it as smooth as possible.

2. Glue the vessel to the smaller cardboard base using a hot glue gun. You want to make sure it is properly stuck down, otherwise it will rise once the silicone is poured and you will ruin your mould.

3. To make the mould wall, cut the larger piece of cardboard into a rectangle that measures a little longer than the widest circumference of your vessel and at least 2 cm (1 in) taller than the height. Press some small folds into the cardboard, to help it bend easily, then use it to encircle the vessel. Make sure there is about 1 cm (½ in) between the wall and vessel all the way around, and glue the bottom edge to the base so it is completely sealed. You don't want any silicone to run out of the join, so make sure it is strong.

4. Follow the packet instructions to mix the two-part silicone in a jug with a spoon. Use your discretion with how much to make, depending on the size of your vessel. The 1:1 ratio silicone we use needs to be mixed for about a minute in a slow, steady motion. If you mix the silicone too fast you will get air bubbles, which will show up in your mould.

5. Once the parts are completely combined in the jug, slowly and steadily pour the silicone into the cardboard mould. Keep your hand steady in one spot and pour from up high to minimise air bubbles. Pour until there's at least 1 cm (½ in) of silicone above the height of the vessel. Leave any excess silicone to dry in the jug – do NOT tip it down the sink! Tap the sides of your freshly poured mould gently for about a minute; this should dislodge any air bubbles in your wet silicone.

→

6. Leave the mould to dry for a minimum of four hours (or follow the packet instructions) – we recommend you let it set overnight for the strongest mould.

7. Once the mould has completely dried, remove the cardboard from the sides and base. You will notice there is a hole in one side of the mould where the bottom of the vessel will be visible – this is the top of your mould and where you will pour wax into later. You want this hole to be neat and round; you may need to cut a little bit of silicone away using a box cutter or scalpel, but be careful to avoid splitting the mould as you do this.

8. Using the scalpel or box cutter, slowly cut a short diagonal line down. Change direction and cut diagonally the other way, and continue in a zig-zag pattern until you can safely wiggle your vessel out pf the seam. Practice doing this gently, as you will be using this technique to pop out your candles. Depending on your vessel, you may need to cut all the way down, or you may only need to cut a small section at the top.

9. Finish the cut with a small horizontal knick with the scalpel or box cutter. This will ensure that when you are pulling your candle out, the silicone won't split any further.

10. Now you will need to make the wick hole. Locate the most central part of the bottom of the mould and prick a hole there with a wooden skewer, going back and forth a few times to ensure a wick can fit through there later. If you have a drill with a small bit handy, you can use this instead.

Making the candle

1. As you may have noticed, you have a big split in the side of your mould, which you will need to seal before you pour your candle so wax doesn't spill out of it. To seal the split, place a bunch of elastic bands tightly around the mould, ensuring the cut seam slots neatly together, as in the picture below. You may be able to see the seam on your candle once it has set (but it will be less noticeable with a textured or unusual shape, so keep this in mind when selecting a vessel).

2. Follow the same instructions for making the Tutti Frutti candle on pages 38–39, gently wiggling the candle out of the seam once it has set.

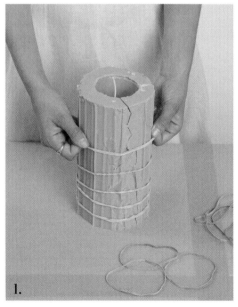

1.

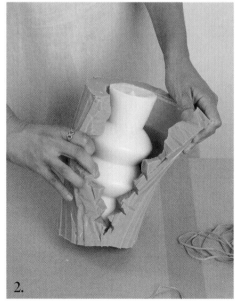

2.

SCENTS OF SELF

SIMPLE SCENTED CANDLE

Creating a scented candle is one of the easiest projects you can do, plus your space will smell delish! We prefer to make our scented candles in a vessel as they last longer – essential oils can be pricey. A free-standing soy wax candle only has around eight hours of burn time, whereas a jar candle can last more than 20 hours. Make your scented candle stand out by using a unique vessel, such as a small vase, a coloured glass, a tea cup, even the rind of your favourite citrus fruit! We buy coloured glasses from second-hand shops, which not only means our candles are interesting but also more sustainable. Etsy is another great place to purchase Murano glass or retro jars.

It's important to weigh your wax when making scented candles as it will help to determine how much essential oils you need to add. If you want a subtle but sweet scent and a lovely warm glow, leave out the essential oils and simply use beeswax for a natural honey fragrance.

Refer to page 13 for tips on burning safety. Don't make a candle in a vessel with any chips or cracks, and cover your candle when not in use to prevent it from getting dusty.

Making the candle

YOU WILL NEED

~ Coated wick

~ Chosen jar or vessel

~ Wick tab (optional)

~ Soy wax or beeswax

~ Essential oils of your choice
(see page 27 for ideas)

! It's important to select the right wick size for your candle (please refer to page 22 for more information). Depending on the size of the jar, you may even need to use two or more wicks. Keep an eye on the flame when burning your candle; if it is hitting the wall of your jar, you may have selected a wick that is too thick. In this case, don't continue burning it – remove the scented wax from the jar and melt it down to reuse it. It is better to try again than to have an unsafe candle burning in your house.

2.

2.

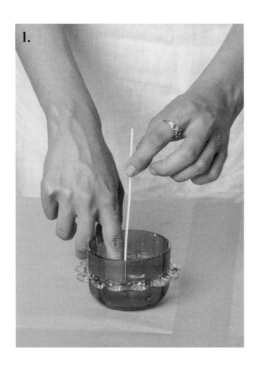

1. Attach the wick to the bottom of your chosen jar or vessel using a wick tab or a tiny amount of hot glue.

2. Place your vessel onto a set of digital scales and zero them. Fill the vessel with wax chips and make a note of the weight, then transfer the wax to a pot. Do this twice as the wax will melt down, calculating the total weight.

3. Melt the wax to the required temperature, checking with a temperature gun and referring to the guide on page 21.

4. Remove the wax from the heat and transfer it to a jug. Using the total weight of the wax from step 2, calculate how much essential oil to use: 15–20 ml to every 500 g of wax (½–¾ fl oz to every 17 oz). When the wax has cooled slightly, add the essential oil, mixing well with a spoon – if the wax is too hot, the oil will burn off.

5. Pour the wax slowly and steadily into your vessel, being careful to keep the wick steady in the centre. Pour to about 2 cm (1 in) below the top of the vessel and ensure plenty of wick is left at the top (it can be trimmed at the end if needed).

6. Secure the wick in the centre of the candle using two popsicle sticks either side of it and a clothes peg to hold it. You can also use a wick-straightening tool. It's important to keep the wick straight for maximum burn time.

7. Let your candle cool at room temperature before burning. Do not refrigerate your scented candle as it can crack the wax.

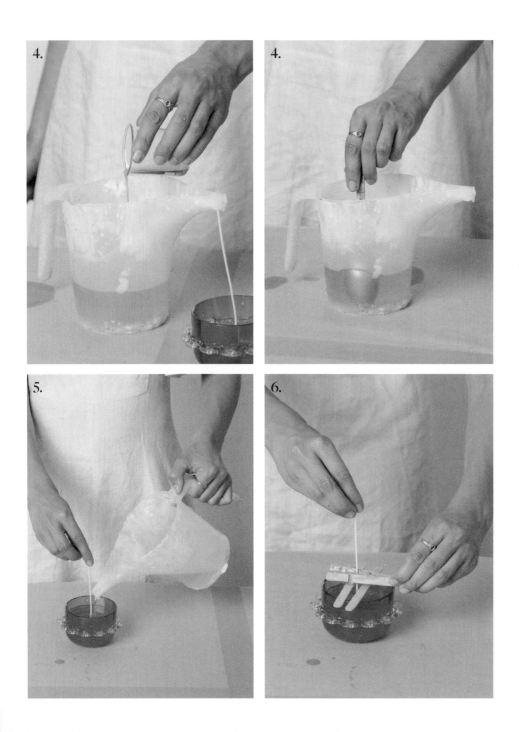

CITRONELLA OUTDOOR CANDLES

Keep the mosquitos away and create a beautiful ambience in your outdoor space with a citronella candle. They smell lovely and will keep you safe from bites. You will need around 3 drops of citronella per 200ml (7 fl oz) of wax.

DINNER PARTY

SIMPLE HAND-DIPPED CANDLE

We love to entertain and share food together, so it's
    important for us to have a candle burning to set the mood.
    Nothing beats cooking up a big feast, decorating the table
    with our eclectic mix of plates, glasses and candelabras,
    and then lighting some of our own beautiful candles.
Taper candles are one of the oldest forms of candle-making.
    You can have a lot of fun creating these misshapen, hand-
    formed candles. We love them because they have so much
    character and are easy to make, and you can get really
    funky with colours and shapes. These will need to be
    placed in a candle holder or candelabra (or see page 62 for
    how to make self-standing hand-dipped candles).

Making the candle

YOU WILL NEED

~ Wax of your choice (we use soy wax or beeswax)

~ Coloured dye of your choice (optional)

~ Wick of your choice (we are using a pre-coated one, but a plain cotton wick will work too)

! We have used a 30 cm (1 ft 12 in) coated wick for this project, but you can go as long as you like – just make sure you can find two vessels that are of similar depth. You can also use a long wick folded in half to make two candles at once! Simply hold the fold when dipping; just be sure to keep the wicks apart as you don't want them to stick together.

1.

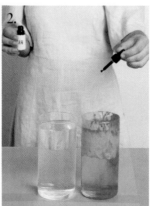

2.

2.

1. Heat the wax in a pot; refer to the wax temperature chart on page 21. Mix the melting wax gently with a spoon, then transfer it to a vessel that is deep enough to fully submerge the wick up to the height you want your candle to be. Fill a vessel of equal size with cold water.

2. If you want to add dye to the wax, do it now, making sure the dye is fully mixed in before you start the dipping process. Alternatively, you can dip-dye the candles at the very end (see page 61 for instructions).

3. Pinching the top of your wick, submerge it in the vessel of wax, leaving at least 3 cm (1 ½ in) out of the wax for you to hold.

4. Remove the wick from the wax, and dip it into the vessel of cool water to harden the wax. Shake as much water off your candle as possible.

5. Repeat steps 3 and 4 until the candle is the desired width. You may need to straighten your candle as you go, but it will be soft and malleable so it is very easy (and we find a slightly bent candle has its own beautiful charm anyway).

6. Once you have achieved the desired candle thickness, peg the candle on a clothes-drying rack or lay it on a flat surface to fully harden.

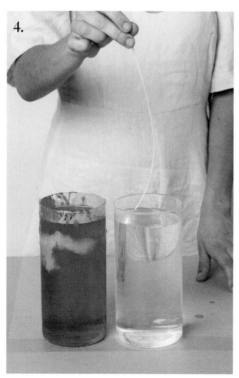
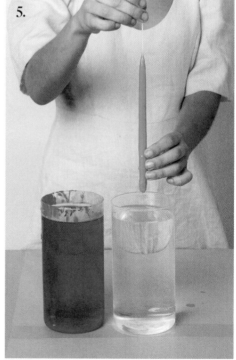

BIRTHDAY CANDLES

Making birthday candles really is going that extra mile for the person you love! These are easy and relatively fast to make – just reduce the scale of this project to make little hand-dipped candles, around 7 cm (2 ½ in) tall. You only need to dip them in the wax a few times and can dip two or even more together.

GROOVY BABY

GRADIENT DIP-DYE CANDLE

If you want to add some colour to your dinner candles, you can brighten them up by dipping them in coloured wax. We use a single colour in this project, but you can get as experimental as you like and go multi-coloured by adding another colour of dye into the wax through the dipping process. Refer to our colour mixing table on page 24 for some great colour combinations.

Making the candle

YOU WILL NEED

~ Wax of your choice (we use soy wax or beeswax)

~ Wick of your choice (we are using a pre-coated one, but a plain cotton wick will work too)

~ Coloured dye of your choice

1. Follow steps 1–4 of the Dinner party candle on page 55, repeating steps 3 and 4 to dip the candle into the wax and water until your candle is half-formed. Peg the candle on a clothes-drying rack.

2. Colour the remaining wax with a small amount of dye. Don't use too much dye as it is the starting point for your gradient. Agan dip the candle into the wax and water (referring to steps 3 and 4 on page 55), trying not to dip to exactly the same line over and over – you want to blur the gradient by dipping to slightly different lines each time.

3. Once you can see the colour appear on your candle, set it aside on your drying rack again, and add a little bit more dye (of the same or different colour) to the wax, ensuring you mix it in well. You really want to go slowly with the addition of dye, as the slower you go, the smoother your gradient will be.

4. Dip your candle again, but this time don't fully submerge it. Stop around 3 cm (1½ in) from the top of your candle so the base colour can still be seen.

5. Repeat steps 3 and 4, each time adding a little bit more dye and dipping less of your candle, so each shade (or different colour) can be seen, from the lightest colour at the top of your candle down to the strongest colour at the base. Peg the candle back on the drying rack to set.

STANDING PROUD

SELF-STANDING HAND-DIPPED CANDLE

If you don't have a candle holder or candelabra but like the look of a hand-dipped candle, then create a candle that will stand on its own! We love making these en masse in different colours, then scattering them on a table setting surrounded by flowers and food. It's very important to make sure the candles stand on their own, so make sure they balance perfectly before lighting up.

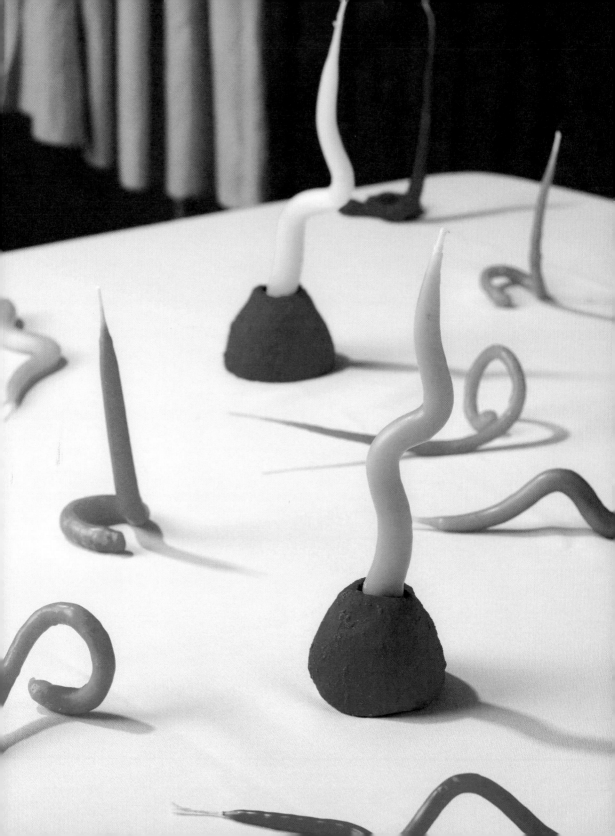

Making the candle

YOU WILL NEED

~ Wax of your choice (we use soy wax or beeswax)

~ Coloured dye of your choice (optional)

~ Wick of your choice (we are using a pre-coated one, but a plain cotton wick will work too)

SHAPE UP

You can use the basis of this technique to create a hand-dipped candle in any shape you like! Wiggle your wick while in the wax so it's wonky like a snake. Tie your wick in knots to give your candle a bulbous effect. Knot the base of your wick into a flower. Or use both ends of the wick to make a U-shaped standing candle.

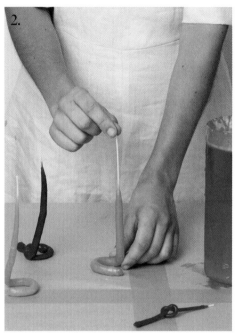
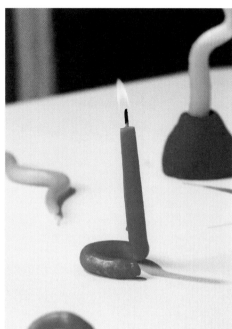

1. Follow steps 1–5 of the Dinner party candle on page 55, adding dye to the wax if you wish.

2. Once you have achieved your desired thickness, take the bottom of the candle and bend it on a 90-degree angle, then curl that part around so it can act as a stand for the main part of your candle. Balance it on a surface to test that it can stand up on its own.

3. Once you are satisfied the candle will stand up, gently put it in a fresh vessel of cold water and hold it in that shape to help set the wax. To further support the candle as it continues to harden, you can rest the base on the table and peg the wick upright to a clothes-drying rack or a dish rack placed on its side.

NEAPOLITAN ICE-CREAM

LAYERED CANDLE

Creating a layered candle gives you the opportunity to play with colours, using any number and combination you like. Our signature pillar candle made from brown, white and pink is one of our favourites; it is a nostalgic reminder of the Neopolitan ice-cream we loved as kids.

You can make a layered candle in a mould or a clear glass jar or vase, as long as you can see the colours of each wax layer once your candle is finished. We suggest an even pour for each layer of this candle, but you can experiment with different amounts of each coloured wax, or even add a different scent to each layer.

This candle will be a test of your patience, as you will need to between each pour. Set up the project in a place where it won't be disturbed and where you can come back to it at intervals. Don't rush the wait time! If you don't wait long enough, your colours will mix together and you won't get lovely distinct layers.

Making
the
candle

YOU WILL NEED

~   Coated wick

~   Mould or clear vessel

~   Wick tab (optional)

~   Wax of your choice (we use a soy wax
    that is suitable for a free-standing candle;
    see page 16 for more information)

~   Coloured dyes of your choice

~   Essential oils of your choice (optional)

!   When you have mixed dyed wax to your
    desired colour, we recommend testing
    a small amount in a paper cup because
    coloured wax can sometimes look
    completely different once it sets.

1. If you are using a mould, thread the wick through the wick hole and centre it. If you are using a clear vessel, attach a wick to the bottom using a wick tab or a tiny amount of hot glue to hold it in place. If you are adding essential oils, weigh your wax before you begin to determine oil quanities, referring to the Scents of self instructions on page 49.

2. Melt your wax to the required temperature (refer to the chart on page 21). Add your choice of coloured dye and mix well until it has melted evenly throughout your wax. (We use brown for the first part to replicate chocolate ice-cream.) Remove wax from heat. If you want to add essential oils, do it after the wax has cooled slightly.

3. Transfer the wax to a jug and pour it into the mould or vessel until it is about a third full – you can estimate this by sight, or you can measure and mark it out with a ruler and tape on the mould or vessel. Take care not to spill any wax on the sides of your mould or vessel, as the colour will show up in the other layers.

4. Secure the wick so it's in the centre of your candle using a clothes peg (and popsicle sticks if needed) or a wick-straightening tool. Allow to set for one hour.

5. Heat the next batch of wax, but use a different coloured dye and/or essential oils. (The second section of our Neapolitan candle is white for vanilla ice-cream, so we don't add any dye this time.) Slowly pour the second section of wax into the mould or vessel until it is about two-thirds full and leave to set for another hour.

6. Heat the last batch of wax using the same method as before. Add the dye and/or essential oils (we use pink for strawberry ice-cream) and fill to the top so the mould or vessel is full.

7. Allow the candle to set for two hours. If using a mould, carefully pull the candle from the mould, and trim the wick if required.

DREAMING OF GREECE

TWO-TONE DIAGONAL CANDLE

Bring a little of the Mediterranean into your home! We love the idea of modernising this classic Ancient Greek column shape by pouring two colours on an angle, but you could use this technique with any mould shape. We use a pre-bought mould for this project; these are readily available on many online stores, including eBay.

Making the candle

YOU WILL NEED

~ Coated wick

~ Ancient Greek column mould (or any other shaped mould)

~ Wax of your choice (we use a soy wax that is suitable for moulds – see page 16 for more information)

~ Coloured dyes of your choice

3.

4.

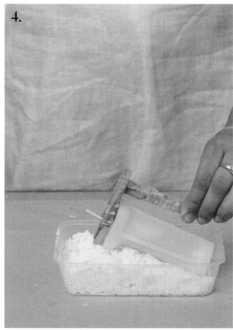

1. Thread the wick through the hole in the base of the mould. Pour some extra wax chips or dry rice into a container bigger than your mould, then rest the mould in the container on a 45-degree angle.

2. Melt half of the wax for the candle in a pot – refer to page 21 for the temperature guide. Add your choice of dye to the wax and stir until it is evenly mixed. (We use 1 drop of brown dye and 1 drop of orange dye to make a light tan colour. Before pouring the wax into your mould, we recommend testing the colour by pouring some into a paper cup and waiting until it sets.)

3. Transfer the melted wax into a jug, then slowly pour it into the mould, until the wax has reached the top of your mould on one side – the diagonal pour should leave room in your mould for a second colour.

4. Take two clothes pegs and make an L-shaped contraption to rest on your mould to hold your wick straight. Allow to set for three hours.

5. Once your first layer has hardened, take the mould out of the container and place it upright.

6. Melt your second batch of wax. If you want to add another colour, do so now. (We leave this part white.) Transfer the second batch of wax into the jug, and slowly fill up the rest of the mould.

7. Secure the wick with a clothes peg again, and allow the candle to harden for another three hours, or until the wax has completely cooled. Then gently pull your candle from the mould, and your lovely diagonal line will be exposed!

BENDING THE RULES

TWISTED DINNER CANDLE

If you have regular dinner candles lying around your house, this is an easy and fun project that will transform them into works of art. Creating twisted candles is really simple – you just need hot water! You can get creative by adding the twist in the centre, at the top or bottom, or by twisting the whole length of the candle.

The candles will need to be made from paraffin wax; other wax, such as soy, will just melt. If you don't have any dinner candles made from paraffin wax at home, you can buy them from the supermarket. You can use coloured candles, or follow the instructions on page 80 to dip-dye the candles once they're twisted.

Making the candle

YOU WILL NEED

~   Dinner candles made from paraffin wax

!   You need to work quickly at steps 3 and 4, before the wax hardens. If you are making a few candles, you can leave them in the water until they are ready to be twisted. If the candle hardens too quickly, just pop it back into your warm water until it is soft again.

3.

4.

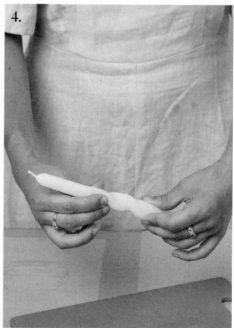

1. Find a jug or container that is at least the same height as your candle, and fill it with warm water from the tap. Check the temperature is around 65 °C (149 °F). If it is too hot you will melt your candle, so be careful!

2. Immerse the candle in the water completely, and let sit for 10–15 minutes or until you can feel your candle is malleable.

3. Remove the candle from the water, and using a jar or rolling pin, gently roll along the length of the candle until it is slightly flattened, leaving the base of the candle in its original form so it will still fit into a candle holder.

4. Gently twist the flattened sections of your candle until you get the desired effect. Have fun and play around with different shapes!

FREE-STANDING U-SHAPED DINNER CANDLE

Follow steps 1 and 2 of this project, then remove your candle from the water and use a jar or rolling pin to roll only the middle third of the candle flat. This will be the base of your free-standing candle, so make sure it's flat enough to support the ends of the candle standing up. Bend both ends of the candle at a 90-degree angle where the rounded candle meets the flattened section, so the candle is a U shape.

You can play around here, flattening a smaller amount of the base or curving up in a more rounded shape – you just have to make sure it's balanced. You can also use a scalpel or box cutter to cut away wax from the wick at the bottom of your candle to burn it from both ends.

COLOUR ME HAPPY

TWO-TONED DIP-DYED CANDLE

This is another easy way to brighten up any sad old dinner
    candles you have lying around your home, or use this
    project to add colour to your twisted candles. Pick a
    couple of colours and go for it!
To keep things simple, you can also dip the candle in one
    colour, leaving the other end white – just melt half the
    amount of wax and stop at step 4.

Making the candle

YOU WILL NEED

~ Wax of your choice (we use soy wax)

~ Coloured dyes of your choice

~ Paraffin wax dinner candles

! If you are using dye chips instead of liquid dye, you will need to keep the wax on the heat while you mix them to help melt them down, meaning you will need to melt the wax for each colour in a seperate pot.

1. Choose two vessels deep enough to dip half your candle, and melt enough wax to fill them both (we use 4 cups of wax). Stir until the wax is melted at the correct temperature – see page 21 for guide.

2. Pour half of the wax into one vessel. Leave the rest in the pot and turn the heat off.

3. Add a few drops of dye to the wax in the vessel to create the colour you desire and mix well. We suggest you go pretty hard with the dye in this step, as a higher pigment will mean less dipping and a stronger colour. (Test colours by pouring some wax into a paper cup and waiting until it hardens.)

4. Hold the candle at one end and dip half or a third (depending on the effect you'd like to create) into your vessel for a few seconds, then take it out. Repeat until your desired colour is achieved, then peg the candle on a clothes-drying rack to set.

5. Pour the remaining wax into the second vessel and add the dye for the second colour, mixing well.

6. Turn the candle around the other way and repeat step 4 using your second colour. You can overlap the colours to create a tri-coloured candle, or leave a gap to let a bit of the white candle shine through. Once you are happy with the effect, peg the candle back on the drying rack to set.

AW SHUCKS

TEALIGHT CANDLE

Tealight candles are a classic in the candle world. They have a cheery and warm aesthetic and are just so cute. Tealight candles can be purchased in bulk at convenience stores, but homemade tea candles allow you to reuse your vessels over and over (which is much better for the environment). Plus you can use any shaped vessel you like, such as a shell!

We learnt this idea from our dear friend Alice. It is so simple, and the candles look amazing scattered down a long table alongside a seafood feast. Since they're so small, you can make lots at the same time – try six or ten.

You can also place your tealight candles in glasses, jars and ceramics to protect them from draughts and to create a lovely glow. Try using coloured glass vessels for a really beautiful look.

Making the candle

YOU WILL NEED

~ Oyster shells (or other small vessels)

~ Coated wicks (suitable for a small candle; see page 22)

~ Wick tabs (optional)

~ Wax of your choice (we use soy wax)

~ Essential oils of your choice (optional)

! To reuse your shells (or other vessels), simply pour boiling water over them until the wax has disappeared. Make sure you do this outside and not over the sink.

1. Thoroughly clean and dry your oyster shells – you don't want any fishy smells! If you are adding essential oils, weigh your wax before you begin to determine oil quanities, referring to the Scents of self instructions on page 49.

2. Cut your wicks to roughly 7 cm (2 ¾ in). Stick a wick to the bottom of each shell using a wick tab or hot glue, ensuring they are nice and straight. Rest each shell in a container of dry rice or extra wax chips to keep them still and upright when you pour.

3. Melt the wax for your candles at the required temperature (refer to page 21 for the temperature guide). You will only need to melt a small amount of wax as oyster shells are tiny. Once the wax has cooled slightly, add any essential oils if you want scented tealights.

4. Transfer the wax into a jug, and pour it carefully into each shell. Secure the wicks in the centre of the candles using a clothes peg or wick-straightening tool. Allow to set for one hour and trim wicks as needed.

C'EST MAGIQUE

MARBLE CANDLE

Marble candles are like magic! You can create your own
swirly, whirly psychedelic candle at home using nail polish
or paint. Disclaimer: this is one of the messier projects in
our book, so take the time to prepare your space, otherwise
you'll end up with nail polish or paint everywhere – and it
isn't as easy as wax to clean up!

Making the candle

YOU WILL NEED

~ A base candle (we use a moulded candle, but a taper or dinner candle will work too)

~ 2–3 x coloured nail polishes or enamel paint colours (found at art stores)

! Nail polish and enamel paint can let off toxic fumes and tend to be a little stinky. It's best to work in an open-air space or even outside for this activity if possible. If you do work inside, make sure your space is fully ventilated with windows or doors open. You may also want to wear gloves to avoid getting paint on your hands, and keep an acetone-based nail polish remover around in case there are any spills.

1. Lay old newspaper or cardboard down in your workspace, allowing for drips and splatters.

2. Fill a bucket or large container with enough water to fully submerge your candles. Then add 3–6 drops of an enamel paint or nail polish into the bucket. Once this first colour has spread across the surface of the water, add the second and third colour (if using) in the same fashion.

3. Using a skewer, spoon or popsicle stick, gently swirl the colour around to create a marbled effect.

4. Hold a candle firmly by the wick and slowly dip it into the bucket, moving the candle around in a quick circular motion. Take the candle out and shake it to remove any excess water.

5. Stand your candle upright on a newspaper- or cardboard-covered surface and peg the wick to a clothes-drying rack, ensuring the wet candle isn't touching any surface. Leave to dry for an hour. Follow these steps for each individual candle you want to marble, using cotton pads or paper towel to remove the old paint or polish before starting again.

VOLCANO SURPRISE

HIDDEN-COLOUR CANDLE

When a candle looks like a piece of art, sometimes people don't want to burn it and instead leave it sitting pretty on a mantle. But here is a candle designed to burn for maximum sculptural effect. Plain white on the outside, this candle contains secret blocks of vivid colour that cascade out in a colourful explosion, changing shape and forming 'rocks' like lava. Every candle will be perfectly unique, only revealing itself once burnt. A great one for dinner parties.

Making the candle

YOU WILL NEED

~ Soy wax (because it changes form and drips like lava)

~ Coloured liquid dyes of your choice (liquid dyes are much easier than hard dyes for this project, as you can mix colours separately after you have melted your wax)

~ Silicone ice-cube tray (make sure the moulds of this tray are small enough to fit in your candle mould)

~ Coated wick

~ Mould of your choice (we use our Dante Candle Mould, aptly named after the fictional volcano Dantes Peak for the way it drips and changes form like a real candle volcano!)

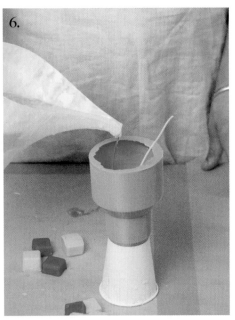

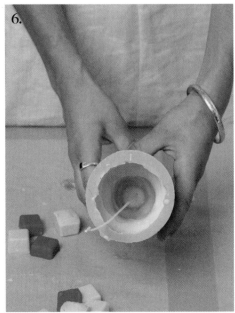

6.

6.

1. Melt a small amount (roughly 2 cups) of soy wax to temperature (refer to page 21), mixing as you go until it has all melted, then pour it into a jug.

2. Set out paper cups or small vessels, one for each colour you want to use, and divide the wax evenly between them.

3. Add a coloured dye to each cup and mix well. You need the pigment to be quite strong, but depending on your dye, one or two drops per cup should work well.

4. Pour the waxes into the silicone ice cube tray to create a few cubes of each colour. You may not use all of them today, but you can store them for next time. Allow them to dry for around two hours, until they are completely hard, then remove them from the tray.

5. Melt enough soy wax for your chosen candle mould, mixing until it has all melted.

6. Thread the wick through the mould, then pour a small amount of the plain undyed wax into the mould and move it around so the wax coats the sides. This will make the outside of your candle white. Repeat a few times until you are satisfied you have a thin layer of wax covering the entirety of your mould.

7. Take your coloured cubes of wax and stack them inside your mould (cutting them smaller if necessary). Think about how you want your candle to melt – if you want your colours to combine (for example, our yellow and pink will make a peach when melted together), place them side by side in the mould. If you would prefer to have single bold colours, stack them on top of each other at varying levels.

8. Pour more undyed melted wax into your mould over the top of the coloured cubes. Depending on the size of your mould you may want to add your coloured and plain wax in a couple of stages – we did our candle in two stages as the mould is quite tall and we wanted to be able to space the colours apart a little bit.

9. Once your mould is full, secure the wick using a clothes peg or wick-straightening tool. Allow the candle to set for approximately four hours, or until your candle has cooled completely, then pull it from the mould.

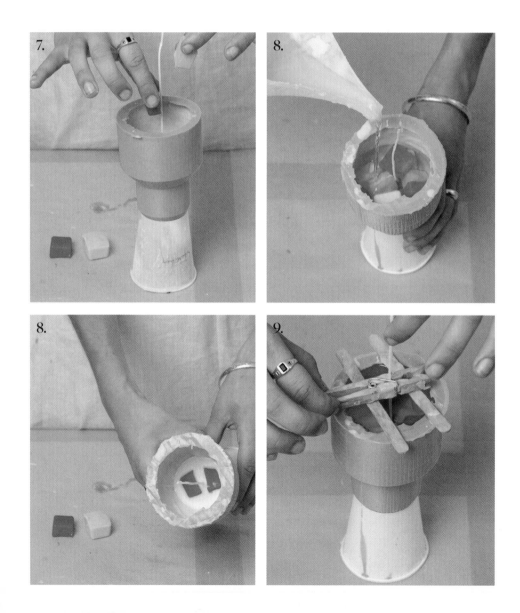

7.

8.

8.

9.

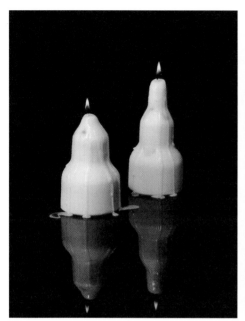

MELLOW

TIE-DYE CANDLE

We are heading way back to the 1960s with this one! Who doesn't love a bit of tie-dye in their life? Light this candle and it will transport you to Woodstock in 1969, listening to Janis Joplin with round, rose-coloured shades on. You can use a candle of any colour or shape for this project. We use a plain white base candle and one colour of dye, but you could use a pale coloured candle and opt for a complementary colour – or colours – for your tie-dye. Anything goes!

Making the candle

YOU WILL NEED

~ Coloured solid dye of your choice

~ A base candle

1.

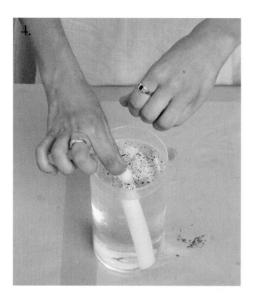

1. Using a scalpel or box cutter, shave about one teaspoon of dye into powder or small chips and set aside.

2. Fill a container or jar, about the same height as your candle, with boiling water from the kettle, and another vessel of a similar size with cold water.

3. Sprinkle a pinch of dye onto the surface of the vessel containing the hot water. The dye will melt and sit on the surface of the water. Experiment with dropping dye in different places, as this will change the way it dyes your candle.

4. Holding your candle by the wick, fully submerge it into the hot water and pull it straight back out again. The dye you have dropped onto the surface will cling to your candle, creating a tie-dye effect.

5. Dip your candle in the vessel containing the cold water to set the dye.

6. Repeat these steps (using the same colour or other colours of dye), until you are happy with the effect. Peg the candle on a clothes-drying rack to set.

SOLID AND STRIPED

WAX SHEET CANDLE

Wax sheets are a great tool for decorating pre-bought candles or plain candles you have made yourself. This method is really fun because you can use your imagination, making geometric patterns, illustrative prints or even three-dimensional shapes (see page 104).

This striped design is very simple and looks great on a straight candle or a candle with an unusual shape, such as our Dante candle. You will get a really cool effect where the stripes spread as they melt and create an optical illusion.

Making the candle

YOU WILL NEED

~   Decorative wax sheets in your chosen colours (we love Stockmar Decorating Wax sheets, which you can buy online)

~   A base candle

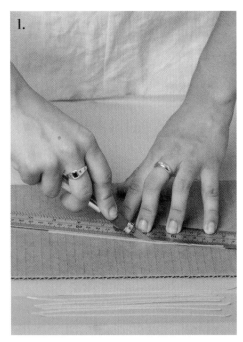

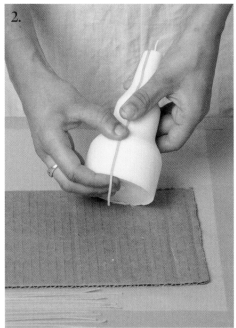

1. Using a ruler, chopping board and scalpel or box cutter, cut 10 strips of the wax sheet around 5 mm (⅕ in) wide and the same length as your candle. (If your candle doesn't have a flat surface, use a piece of string to roughly measure out the length, placing it on the surface of the candle, then straightening it out against a ruler. If in doubt, give yourself some extra length as you can always trim any extra wax off the bottom once it is stuck.) Try to keep the strips uniform for the most effective result.

2. Wax sheets are easiest to use when they are warmed up a bit, so soften the strips a little in your hands. Neatly place the first strip of wax on the candle in a vertical direction and apply pressure with your fingers until it's stuck the entire length of the candle.

3. Turn the candle over and repeat step 2 on the opposite side, so the stripes mirror each other.

4. Continue to place the stripes evenly around your candle until you are happy with the effect. You may need to cut more strips to fill your candle.

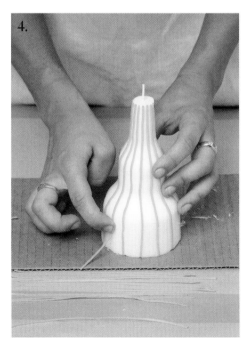

4.

TI AMO

Wax sheets are so versatile, allowing you to create many different patterns. We love to decorate white candles with lots of small hearts. Flowers, clouds, stars and fruit look great too. Or you can try to create a simple scene, such as a sun in the sky and an ocean. Use a fine marker or pencil to draw your shapes onto the back of your wax sheets and small manicure scissors to cut them out, then apply pressure with your fingers to stick them to the base candle.

GARDEN OF EDEN

THREE-DIMENSIONAL FLOWER CANDLE

We searched high and low on our trip to Mexico for a
   particular Oaxacan ornate flower candle, and one day
   in a random shop we looked up to discover the whole
   ceiling was hung with them. We almost swapped out our
   boyfriends' seats on the plane to bring them home!
This is a version of that candle you can make at home with
   wax sheets. While it is a fiddly process, it is the most
   effective way of using wax sheets to decorate your candle,
   as you get a 3D effect. You can experiment with different
   petal and leaf shapes.

Making the candle

YOU WILL NEED

~ Decorative wax sheets in your chosen colours

~ A base candle

! If you are having trouble making your petals stick, your wax may not be warm enough. Remember to warm the wax in your hands before sticking it onto the candle, or work in front of a heater. If all else fails, take small pins and insert them through the whole 3D sculpture to affix to the candle base.

1. Draw your desired shapes onto your wax sheets using a fine marker or pencil. For each candle, we made two flowers, each with a larger and smaller petal shape, two leaf shapes, and a round centre. Use contrasting colours for each shape, or all the same for a monochrome effect. If you'd like to keep the shapes really consistent for each flower, you can create a stencil to trace.

2. Cut out the shapes using small manicure scissors, a box cutter or scalpel.

3. Take the larger wax petal shape and mould the petals, curling them with your fingers to sit slightly upright. Warm the wax in your hands, then press the centre of the shape firmly into your candle, using the pressure and warmth of your fingers to set the wax.

4. Take the two leaves and slip them in between the large petal shape and the candle. Wedge them in and gently press until they are stuck.

5. Push your round centre into the middle of the smaller petal shape until it is stuck, then mould the smaller petal shape in the palm of your hand to form the inner section of your flower, shaping it into a little cup. Press and fix this to the centre of your larger petal shape to complete your flower.

BRUSH STROKES

PAINTED CANDLE

Hand painting is a wonderful way to brighten up regular
store-bought candles. They are perfect for themed dinner
parties or as a gift. Plan your design before you begin; using
contrasting colours can be really striking. Repetition is
key with this project, and paper stencils can be an effective
way to achieve this – you can even create your own using
masking tape.

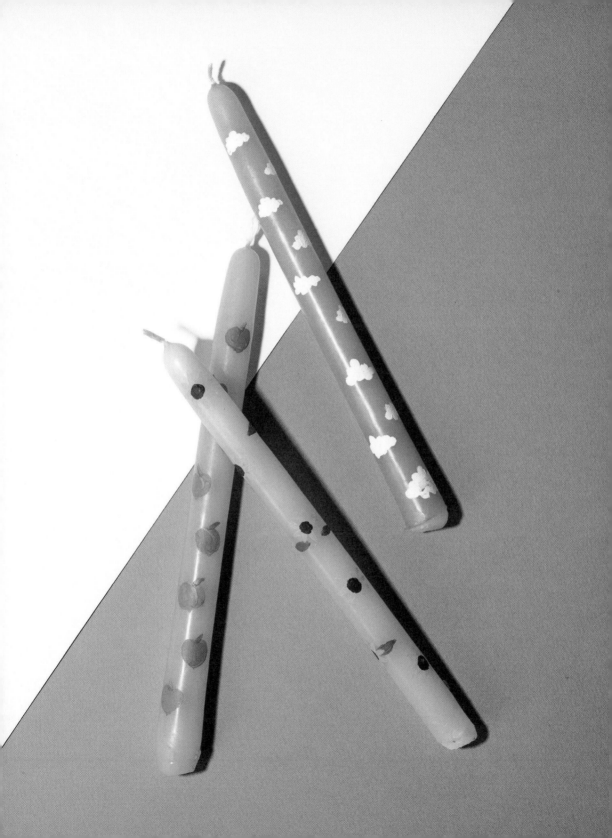

Making the candle

YOU WILL NEED

~ A base candle (we use paraffin wax candles, but this will also look great on other types of candles)

~ Nail polish remover and cotton wipes

~ Fine paint brush

~ Acrylic paints of your choice

! Decorating your candle with acrylic paint is safe, but you must ensure you only paint the outside of the candle – do not paint around the wick. While burning, keep an eye on your painted candles, like all candles. We recommend not painting too heavily or thickly with this technique to avoid fire hazards. Please ensure you wait an hour or two before burning to make sure the paint is fully dried.

1. First clean your candle using nail polish remover and cotton wipes.

2. Start painting at least 1 cm (½ inch) from the top of the candle. You can paint any design you like on your candles; we've done sunflowers (yellow, green and brown paint on a pink candle), peaches (orange and green on a yellow candle) and clouds (white on a blue candle). You could cut a shape out of paper to create a stencil if you would like to keep the designs consistent.

3. Peg the candle on a clothes-drying rack and let the first coat completely dry before applying a second or third coat as required, washing out your brush thoroughly before using different paint colours.

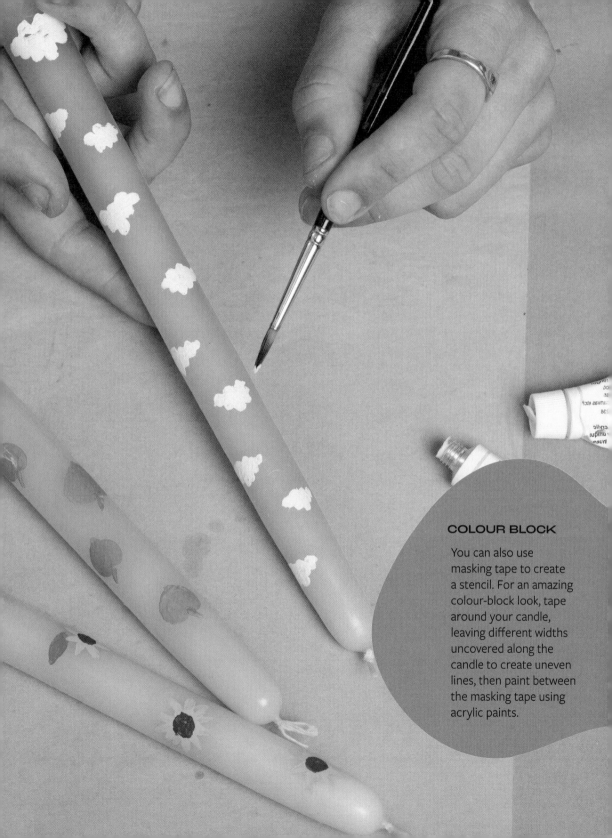

COLOUR BLOCK

You can also use masking tape to create a stencil. For an amazing colour-block look, tape around your candle, leaving different widths uncovered along the candle to create uneven lines, then paint between the masking tape using acrylic paints.

BIG DIPPER

MULTI-WICK CANDLE

Do you have a bowl that you just LOVE? This is the perfect
project to double the function of your favourite ceramic by
turning it into a multi-wick candle you can display on any
occasion. We have had the most success using a bowl that is
wide and shallow.

Making the candle

YOU WILL NEED

~ 3–6 x coated wicks, depending on the size of your bowl

~ Ceramic/heatproof bowl

~ Rulers or strips of cardboard wider than the diameter of your bowl

~ Wax of your choice (we use soy, but beeswax would be lovely too)

~ Essential oils of your choice (optional)

1. First you will need to work out how many wicks you need for your bowl. Refer to the wick guide on page 22. Our wicks were made for a candle jar with a diameter of 10 cm (4 in). As our bowl has a diameter of 30 cm (12 in), we could fit three wicks across the bowl each way, so we used five wicks in total. Plan to evenly space them around the bowl.

2. Once you have figured out the number and placement of your wicks, use a tiny amount of hot glue on the base of the bowl to hold them in place.

3. Lay your rulers or cardboard strips across the bowl so that they sit next to your wicks, allowing you to peg the wicks upright while resting the pegs on the rulers/cardboard.

4. If you are adding essential oils, weigh your wax to determine oil quanities, referring to the Scents of self instructions on page 49. Melt your wax to the required temperature (refer to our chart on page 21). Add any essential oils after the wax has cooled slightly, mixing well with a spoon.

5. Transfer the wax to a jug and pour into the bowl. Allow to set before trimming the wicks.

AQUATIC BEAUTY

WATER CANDLE

More than candles, these are sculptural works of art. This
is a seriously fun project where you can get amazing and
varied results. It's surprisingly simple and you don't need a
lot of tools, as you use a dinner candle for the base. Be sure
to take care though, as you will be pouring hot wax close to
your hands!

Making the candle

YOU WILL NEED

~ Wax of your choice

~ Coloured dye of your choice (optional)

~ Plate with an upturned lip for affixing your candle (you can also use a jar lid)

~ Dinner candle

1. Fill a large bucket (deep enough to submerge your candle) with cold water.

2. Melt a small amount (roughly 2 cups) of wax at the required temperature (refer to page 21 for the temperature guide). Add some dye if you want a coloured candle and mix well. Pour the wax into a jug, then pour a little wax onto the plate.

3. Push the base of the candle into the wax, then dip your plate and attached candle in the bucket of water to cool the wax and make it harder, securing the candle. Pour more wax around the edges and dip the plate and candle into the water as many times as necessary to ensure the candle is stuck on properly.

4. Hold the plate in one hand over the bucket of water. Carefully pour a splash of wax onto the plate, until it is almost overflowing. Slowly submerge the base of the plate in the water until you see the wax begin to set in an amazing shape.

5. While the plate is still in the water, keep pouring the wax, as close to your candle as possible so the wax grabs hold of the candle as you pour. Submerge more and more of the candle, gently moving the plate up and down to get different shapes, until you are happy with the effect. You can display your candle on your plate, or carefully remove it once it's set to become a freestanding candle.

THE QUEEN BEE

MULTI-CANDLE CENTREPIECE

This is the mother of all candles, a project you can really go
   bananas with. We love making these when we have lots
   of spare candles lying around – maybe the ones that have
   funny marks or chips on them – to create one dramatic
   centrepiece! If you don't have spare candles lying around,
   that's fine too. Prepare a bunch of candles using a few
   moulds of varying heights. You can also just buy some
   candles – but make sure they are made from the same type
   of wax.

Making *the* candle

YOU WILL NEED

~   5 or more candles of varying heights,
    made from the same wax

~   Wax (preferably the same type of wax
    that your existing candles are made of)

~   Coloured dye of your choice (optional)

1. Arrange the candles in a large heatproof
    bowl or pot. Place any taller candles in
    the centre and smaller ones around the
    outside.

2. Heat the wax to the required
    temperature (refer to page 21) and mix
    well. Add coloured dye if you wish.

3. Transfer the wax to a jug and gently pour
    it into the bowl around the base of your
    candles. Try to pour from one spot and
    do it slowly, as the hot wax may melt
    some of your candles a little.

4. Allow to set for four hours. Remove your
    candle from the pot or bowl and voila!

PART THREE

IT'S CALLED STYLING, DARLING

The best thing about candles, in particular the sculptural
ones you have made yourself, is that they are art. They are
sculptures that you can create in any form you like, in any
colour you like, with a low price tag. Styling your home and
your new candle collection will quickly become a fun new
project in itself.

We have always taken such pride in the home that we have
built together over the years. We've filled it with a mixture
of eclectic vintage pieces, modern artworks purchased
from local artists and creators, and trinkets from overseas
travels. A lot of our free time is spent searching our
favourite antique stores and rummaging through garage
sales, and you can see this reflected in our house. We love
how candles – and candle holders – form part of this.

CREATING CLUSTERS

When curating your pieces, it's about finding the perfect balance of things that shine on their own, or finding items that lift each other up when placed together. Decorating your home with groups of candles on a bookshelf, mantlepiece or coffee table is a strong aesthetic. It can look really lovely to create a cluster of three candles of different heights, shapes and sizes, alongside some other ornaments, flowers, art or books. The colours can be all neutrals or all brights, or you can even choose three clashing shades for a striking look in any corner of your home.

MAKING SCENTS

Scented candles are perfect for your bedroom, and create a calming environment for you to relax. They also work really well in the bathroom with a bunch of flowers, on top of your toilet or by the bath. Citronella candles look gorgeous on an outdoor table, and are ideal for a balmy night to keep the bugs away. They will give off a gentle glow that is guaranteed to enhance the ambience of your outdoor area.

CREATIVE CANDLE-MAKING

You can try many different methods of decorating a candle even once it's complete, such as dripping wax on top of it or dipping it in more wax to create something unique and intriguing. Stacking new soy candles on top of old ones and burning them can create an ever-changing candle masterpiece.

SETTING THE TABLE

We both come from homes where the ritual of sitting down for a meal together is an important one. Our families would never eat in front of the TV or on the couch. The tablecloth would be put out (the good one if guests were over), the plates and cutlery laid. Dressing our table was more than a quick thing; it became something we enjoyed doing – picking flowers, selecting crockery to match, and lighting the candles.

When we are setting the table for a small gathering we love to use our candelabras and dinner candle holders. This creates an intimate mood, which is perfect for entertaining. We recommend two or three dinner candles are displayed in the centre of the table. When you start adding more than this, it becomes hard to see across the table to speak to your friends.

When we are setting the table for big celebrations such as parties, we like to go with smaller arrangements on the table. Tealight or oyster shell candles nestled in jars or glasses are perfect for this situation, especially if you are seated outside as they will be protected from wind.

CANDLE HOLDERS

We have a big collection of found and purchased candelabras at home. We love to mix our amazing vintage finds with modern candle holders. When searching for the perfect candelabra, a great tip is to look beyond the colour and find one with a great shape. You can easily spray paint your candelabra, or sand it back to change the entire look.

If you like single-candle holders you can arrange different ones together, which will create a fabulous eclectic look, especially scattered in abundance on the dinner table in various shapes and sizes with mismatched plates and cups. If you're more of a minimalist, get some white, black or grey spray paint and turn your candle holders monotone to match.

An Italian carafe bottle is the perfect piece to upcycle into a candle holder. Go to your local shop and buy a little fat bottle of wine or oil, and once it's empty you'll have a *Lady and the Tramp* setting for you and your date to smooch over spaghetti.

But what better way to display your homemade candles than with a homemade candle holder? We've got some projects to get you started in the next few pages.

BEAUTY IS IN THE EYE OF THE BEHOLDER

CLAY CANDLE HOLDERS

Now that you have all your beautiful new candles, you will need something to hold them! Working with clay is a really meditative process – it's a wonderful exercise to take time for yourself and build things with your hands. The beauty of clay is you can make any shape you like, and then use the base of your dinner candle to imprint its exact size so it sits snugly in there.

Air-dry clay is really simple and easy to use at home. It does not need to be fired in a kiln – just leave it to air dry! You can also use polymer clay, which is baked in the oven.

Remember to just use these shapes and ideas as a guide, because you can get as creative and wacky as you like! You can add spikes, thorns, twists, curls, anything you like. Just ensure the holders will stand up on their own and have ample support at the base to hold your candle upright.

Have fun painting your pieces once they are dry! You can use any type of acrylic paint, and if you add baking soda to your paint before you apply it, you will be left with an amazing rustic ceramic texture, without having to glaze your piece.

YOU WILL NEED

~ Air-dry clay

~ Dinner candle

~ Baking paper

~ Canola oil spray

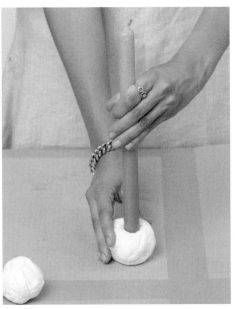
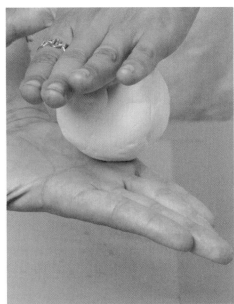

AIR-DRY CLAY TIPS

Prepare your workspace – work with clay on a cutting board or on a plate.

Knead your air-dry clay to warm it up as it will make the clay more malleable and easier to work with.

Use water and your fingers to smooth out any bumps once you have finished moulding your candle holder, but be sparing with the water, as excess will create cracks.

Keep your project strong and sturdy by not making it too thin.

Sand your holders for a smoother finish. This will eliminate any fingerprints or marks. Make sure you wear a mask for this step, as particles from your clay can be harmful to breathe in.

Save leftover clay in an air-tight zip-lock bag.

HONEY POT

SIMPLE BALL CANDLE HOLDER

Make two of these so you have matching holders to pop at each end of your dinner table! Pictured on pages 96 and 135.

1. Take a small amount of clay, about the size of a table tennis ball. Knead it for about one minute until it's soft, then roll it into a perfect ball.

2. Place your ball on a flat surface and use the base of your dinner candle to create an indentation about 2–3 cm (¾–1¼ in) in the ball – deep enough to hold your candle upright. This will also naturally flatten the bottom of the ball so that it can stand on a surface.

3. Remove your candle and let the clay dry according to packet instructions, on baking paper sprayed with canola oil.

! You can stack multiple clay balls on top of each other to achieve more height with your candle holder. Simply use a knife to score the surface of the balls with small cross hatches where they will be joined, then make some slip of equal parts water and clay as glue to join them together. Be sure to press the candle into your top ball before joining them together, so you don't squash the entire structure when you do it.

THE HOMER

DONUT CANDLE HOLDER

You can make this candle holder to display multiple candles at once; these instructions make one that fits three, as pictured on page 18. It's important to space the holes for the dinner candles evenly so that the holder stands upright when the candles are burning.

1. Take a small amount of clay, about the size of a tennis ball. Knead it for about one minute until it's soft, then roll it into a ball.

2. Use the palms of your hands to roll the ball into a sausage around 4 cm (1 ½ in) in diameter. Try to keep the sausage an even thickness all the way along, rolling until it reaches a length of 15–20 cm (6–8 in).

3. Slice the ends so they are smooth and score each end with your knife (creating small cross hatches). Use a little water to dab the ends, then press them together and blend the seam with your finger so it is smooth.

4. Take a regular-sized dinner candle and press three holes about 2–3 cm (¾–1 ¼ in) deep at evenly spaced intervals into the donut.

5. Let the clay dry according to packet instructions, on baking paper sprayed with canola oil.

UPSIDE

U-SHAPED CANDLE HOLDER

Elevate your candles with this U-shaped mini candelabra, pictured on page 79.

1. Take a small amount of clay, about the size of a tennis ball. Knead it for about one minute until it's soft, then roll it into a ball.

2. Use the palms of your hands to roll the ball into a sausage around 4 cm (1 ½ in) in diameter. Try to keep the sausage an even thickness all the way along, rolling until it reaches a length of 15–20 cm (6–8 in).

3. Bend the clay into a U shape, and gently press the curved edge onto your work surface to flatten it so that the candle holder will stand without wobbling.

4. Take your dinner candle and gently press down into the two ends of the holder to make two indents, about 2–3 cm (¾–1 ¼ in) deep.

5. Let the clay dry according to packet instructions, on baking paper sprayed with canola oil.

SAVE OUR SURFACES
CANDLE TRAY

If you have made sculptural soy wax candles from any of the projects in this book, you will know that the wax melts in a beautiful volcanic way – but sometimes it can get messy. Here is a simple tray to protect your surfaces from drippy soy wax, pictured on page 18.

1. Take a small amount of clay, about the size of a tennis ball. Knead it for about one minute until it's soft, then roll it into a ball.

2. Use a jar or rolling pin to roll out the clay until it's a flat cirlce. You can also cut the flattened clay into a shape (think about how many candles you want to fit on it or where the tray will sit in your home). Make sure you account for some extra space around the edge of the shape so you can build up the sides.

3. Using your fingers, mould the edge of the tray to create a curved lip, which will stop any wax from dripping over onto your furniture.

4. Once you are happy with the shape of your tray, allow it to dry according to packet instructions, on baking paper sprayed with canola oil.

PLASTER OF PARIS

CANDLE HOLDER

If air-dry clay isn't your thing, plaster sure will be! Plaster is a fun medium to work with – you can create on a larger scale and also get more adventurous. This project uses a cup as a mould, but you could use almost anything, and you can also experiment with dying the plaster using paint. Plaster candle holders are great outdoors as they are sturdy and won't blow away in the wind.

Making the holder

YOU WILL NEED

~   Paper cup

~   Petroleum jelly

~   Plaster of Paris

~   Disposable container

~   Paint (optional)

~   Dinner candle

1. Cover your work surface with newspaper or cardboard, and use your finger to brush the inside of your paper cup with petroleum jelly, which will help when it's time to remove the plaster.

2. Mix up a small amount of Plaster of Paris with water in a disposable container according to the packet instructions (most require a 2:1 ratio of plaster to water). Slowly add the water and mix well with a spoon – don't mix Plaster of Paris with your bare hands. Add a drop of paint if you want to colour the plaster. Try to get the consistency smooth and even, and to mix in the paint really well.

3. Pour the plaster into the prepared paper cup, up to the height that you would like for your candle holder. Tap the cup gently on the table to bring any air bubbles to the surface.

4. Press your dinner candle into the plaster, creating an imprint of the candle. Hold it there for about five minutes until the plaster has begun to set and the candle will stand up on its own. (If you don't want to hold the candle for five minutes, get a thick piece of cardboard and cut out a circular hole the same width as your candle. After you have poured the plaster into the cup, sticky tape the cardboard to the outside of the mould, centering the hole over the opening, and then slide the candle through.)

5. Place the candle holder somewhere safe and out of the weather for 24 hours to dry. You can repeat the steps with other cups until you have used up all your plaster. Once the plaster is dry, gently wiggle the plaster out of the cup and gently sand the edges with sandpaper if you'd like to create a smoother finish.

Acknowledgements

We would like to acknowledge the Traditional Owners of this land where we work and live, the Wurundjeri people of the Kulin nation, and pay our respects to their Elders past, present and future.

Thank you to our beautiful studio friends Megan, Sisi, Alice and Katie for letting us make a mess and always sharing great ideas with us while we are knee-deep in wax.

Thanks to our beautiful family members Melissa, George, Pink, Frederika, Nino, Dom, Connie, Lisa, Gaethan, Jed and Josh for always supporting our creative dreams.

We would also love to thank all the incredible female creatives who loaned us their works for the book: Lifeslice, Rittle, Trinket Solo, Kirsten Perry, Alice McIntosh, Sundborn Ceramics, Mellow, Nicole Lawrence, Tantri Mustika, Isadora Vaughan, and Peacheslacreme for the cake.

Published in 2022 by Hardie Grant Books, an imprint of Hardie Grant Publishing

Hardie Grant Books (Melbourne)
Wurundjeri Country
Building 1, 658 Church Street
Richmond, Victoria 3121

Hardie Grant Books (London)
5th & 6th Floors
52–54 Southwark Street
London SE1 1UN

hardiegrantbooks.com

Hardie Grant acknowledges the Traditional Owners of the country on which we work, the Wurundjeri people of the Kulin nation and the Gadigal people of the Eora nation, and recognises their continuing connection to the land, waters and culture. We pay our respects to their Elders past and present.

A catalogue record for this book is available from the National Library of Australia

Blazed Wax
ISBN 978 1 74379 839 3

10 9 8 7 6 5 4 3 2 1

Commissioning Editor: Emily Hart
Editor: Megan Arkinstall
Design Manager: Kristin Thomas
Designer: George Saad
Stylist: Bridget Wald
Production Manager: Todd Rechner
Production Coordinator: Jessica Harvie

Colour reproduction by Splitting Image Colour Studio
Printed in China by Leo Paper Products LTD.

The paper this book is printed on is from FSC®-certified forests and other sources. FSC® promotes environmentally responsible, socially beneficial and economically viable management of the world's forests.